Plain
Drink
Tea

thank you!
Ward Stothers

Plain Drink Tea

Ward J. Stothers' Book
of Poems and Prayers

The Dungarvon Press, Belfast

ISBN-13: 978-1-496-15456-9

The Dungarvon Press, Belfast
First Edition

Photographs pages 61, 68, 84, 101, 147 by Marda Quon Stothers.
Illustration page 19 from a watercolor by McCall Gilfillan.
Illustration page 130 from a linocut by Merve Jones.

Set in Adobe Garamond Pro, a typeface based on roman types cut by
Jean Jannon in 1615. Jannon followed the designs of
Claude Garamond, which in turn were based on those used by
Aldus Manutius in 1495.

CONTENTS

FORWARD

Who is Ward Stothers? Or more importantly, what is he about? Who is he serving and why might one say of his poems and prayers, "write on!" Read on and you too will discover his carefully crafted verse — not the old play-it-safe kind of sermon but a veritable jungle of words. Risky wisdom for a wild world.

If you are a newcomer to Ward's diction you will be introduced to a message that is "old but ever new." It might not be trendy but is unique in style.

Ward writes from heart and brain to heart and brain. Engaging sounds are pleasing to the ear, warming to the heart, but also unsettling, unnerving, sobering.

In this collection Ward lays out his stall — a challenge and a call. The result? Liquid language. Distilled communication. Single malt Stothers!

Bill McKnight
2014

INTRODUCTION

I have a poetic eye for words. Every spoken sentence could be a poem. Many of my words have been locked away in notebooks, on typed up sheets of paper and in computer files. Living in Belfast amongst so many gifted writers has prompted me to publish my work with the purpose to make available poetic communications of a life journey, providing artistic light for Belfast, Northern Ireland, and other places where a fresh way to peace is needed. When the poems are read aloud, they are heard as welcomed truth. Silently, they mend our hearts and invite our feet to move in rhythm.

Poems are about tangible people, places and things. The poems are also about visions, ways of seeing new language and remembering. My prayers are packaged and addressed to the creator God. Some prayers are poetic; some poems point to God.

I want to create wagons to carry readers beyond today's trouble, the tyranny of the past, and the lurking fear of the future. To make public words of one sojourner celebrating hope. Peace within divided Belfast will transform the Irish and Scots-Irish diasporas, give new emigrants a life full vision and remind the remainder of the resounding success.

My prayers and poems communicate a way of conversing in the world of a personal God. Prayer is simple and deep, talking to and hearing from God. The lights switch on when one or both converse in a relationship for the two together in unity, "Hands juggling souls of glass, shaking, begging, for a place to rest."

A few of the prayers are private personal prayers but most were written for public or group use. They were read aloud to lead people together to honor the curator God.

The wordy text is uniquely mine. We talk to one another. Some chitter, some ponder. To enhance our lives we communicate with people who have different life experiences and come from different cultures. My poems are observations made along the way of a long life. The goal of the book is to guide people seeking to go boldly along an unfolding path.

Hundreds of books have been written on, and because of, the Troubles, Ireland and peace. It is time for less analysis, soul searching and noisome venting. It is time for more elusive nuanced art.

Belfast is lived out within a spray of rattling toughness. It reeks of the finality of death and applauds with an adherence to the institutions of normal everyday living. Life has changed. Journey dreams. Counting friends. Facing mortality. Peace lived; peace loved. The city looks attractive but the aura darkens quickly. Only hope persists and a new day every day.

Our character is shaped by who we are, our history and our vision. Let these words wash over you like warm rain, washing you clean for a fresh tomorrow.

Ward J. Stothers
Belfast, Northern Ireland
2014

Plain
Drink
Tea

CALL TO WORSHIP

This introductory prayer is our honor
for the grave-robbing God
who elbowed aside the permanence of death,
who sits on God's right hand, itching to return
and sup with us, on recreated earth.

We praise you, we worship and adore you.
You hold the heavens in your hand
as stars bow to your fitting palms.
You come in the sunrise and the song of day-start
and bless the splendor of the noon day.
At sunset you sip tea with the dunking
of light as your wheat wafer.

The stars in their courses magnify you.
Day and night startle at your glory.
Your peace blows over the earth
and reconciliation becomes air itself.
The breath of your mouth fills all space.

Time stops short for your sway,
a watchful walk
in the heat of day.
Coursed by your architecting
everything personal in your care.

Your voice comes as the thunder of the storm
and the song of the wind whispers
the appearing of your majesty.
You satisfy all things living, with your abundance
and our hearts, revere in your presence.

Accept us, your willing worshipers, O God.
Turn your face downward, a little, with blessing
and accept our cries of adoration.
From forever when, at forever now,
then forever will be.
God for us, God gracious, God only.

GLORY
THE SHINE OF GOD'S NATURE

Let Glory be for the Father
Who draws us with vacuuming love
Pleads with our insanity and what we claim as reason
Adopts us as God's own.

Sing Glory to the Son
Who has called and collected us as His people
Through the redeeming course of blood
In the scandalous death of God
As Jesus Christ our Savior.

Rain Glory with the Spirit
Pouring God's pitcher of health on thirsting love
Filling hearts with abiding peace
Showering joy on worrisome earth.

God of all Glories
In union as One
Sharing love within your Trinity
Showing life to all your world
Grant us your grace that we may return your Glory.

FRIEND AND ENEMIES

God, You've gone too far —
How could You call us to do,
The impossible?
We love You and You know it but
Loving our enemies!
You know, those ones we have
Especially etched above our brows
And jaw and echo in our inner ears,
With big, bull voices
And scowls for a handshake.

I refuse to be used
This way.
Jonah was right,
The opposite direction is a quiet seashore.
On the Mediterranean
With carping seagulls the only fight to attend.
Will these kind of people hear and hallelujah
And grow your church?

Your request is like being a lamb
Going to the slaughter.
Like asking Heaven
To be lowered down
Involved in pain, suffering and even death.

Endless embarrassment and catcalls
And laughter too
From stoning, faithless bystanders
Swimming in their accurate ignorance.

No one signs up to be last
On the bread line.
Maybe not the first but never the last.
What good comes out of
Offering life to those
Who spit on your kindness
And wail arrogantly in our faces
Heckling our disunity and broken promises.

Are You a God who just can't say no
Over the squalor of sin and torque of brokenness
Who has to make it right
No matter what course rejection
Leaves the lips of a slurring humanity?
Do You want to save the whole — damned world?

Could You be more caring
Than we could imagine? Would You go so far as
To slide off your heavenly throne
And land, dancing on a manger in Bethlehem?
Will You heal and romp
In earthen fettered urban ghettos,
Offering the poor a seat — at your table?

Do You love so much, God,
That life itself
Is given back, free and in the Spirit,
Paid by the purchase of Christ
For us all who breathed,
And once lived, cursing life as —
Enemies of God.

Just tell us Lord where to go,
And we will mount horses
Unstoppable
Learn to ride like a silver streak,
Carrying your love everywhere,
For You are our peace, Jesus,
Breaking down the walls of separation
Leaning over into your creation,
Coveting the wellness of your world
Calling us friend.

WOMEN

Lord, we thank You, today
For the world of women garnished with children
Filling the family scripts of the everyday.

Combing strands of life, parting history
Spinning tales for pausing, toddler breath
Catching up with scurrying, giggling feet.

Guiding teenage trials with tears of healing promise
Praying stormy times through
From stand-still to sit down.
Being the collect call for grown-up tales
Offering the taste of hope for their tied-up lives.

Laboring, loving, lecturing, governing
Banker, lawyer, artist, president.
Co-keeper of the home.

Celebrating each birthday, singing every song
Reading every novel, rehearsing all encouragement
Receipts of love for every gandered rose
Catching kisses from always busy sons
Given squeeze from distant loving daughters
And awe from ever open-mouth husbands.

God, we pray
In the midst of the batter of sin
And shortened wholeness in relationships
That family will mean a wholesome place
For the blessing of mothers, this lifetime.

BENEDICTION

God of grace, good God of bounty
Send us forth to flow your rivers
Reflecting your greatness
In foundations of always, wholeness.

CREATION

Dear God
You announce to us in Jeremiah
That You fill heaven and earth.
Your small toe scrapes across the Gobi in China,
Your foot stretches to Mars;
Handles and partakes of life everywhere
As creation's gardener.

Yet You live not on the canvas of being
But beyond even the corner of its frame;
Your compass is love.
You see everyone and everything
In one meandering drama of unfurling humanity.
Not peeking to know us but knowing to shepherd us
Redeeming and elating your earth.

Would You, God, enliven us,
Here, now, to chase
Your incarnational breeze,
Quench our tireless thirst
Sample your words
Believe your promises.
Tear for understanding
On that which we may do.

In good and wholesome ventures
With mission and purpose.
Behind your steps
To redeem all,
Close and far away,
For your daily glory
As the God who loves us.

PEACE POEMS

PEACE

 Our work in Northern Ireland is to seek the way of peace. Peace is contentment. It is knowing that you have done, are doing and will be able to keep doing good.

After living our whole lives in the urban American cities of Los Angeles and the Bronx New York, and in the San Francisco Bay area, Northern Ireland is a throwback to the safety of the 1950s. With an average 23 homicides a year in a population of one million eight hundred thousand people with a thoroughly Christian ethos and the weariness of the violence, the country is now very safe. Therefore it feels peaceful. We live in the mid-Shankill, a neighborhood community with mom and pop shops, butchers, green grocers, bakeries, cafes, churches and social outreach centers.

So what is peace? The absence of warfare. It is the ability for children to safely walk to school with their siblings and mates, greeted by the crossing guard. The crossing guard is a local person who picks you up after you have tripped on the curb and gashed the bridge of your nose and offers to drive you across to your house. Peace is greeting your neighbor and saying, "I know your sister from the Together Stronger choir. How is she?" "Oh aye, she's grand." Neighborly conversations.

Peace is enhanced by intentionally making a friend from another part of the society with the goal of becoming real friends. These actions alleviate subliminal fears. Telling wee stories about your friendship adds to the integration.

In the introduction I said "Peace within divided Belfast will transform the Irish and Scots-Irish diasporas, give new emigrants a life full vision, and remind the remainder of the resounding success." It has been many years since the Good Friday Agreement of 1998, and decommissioning of weapons by the IRA and Loyalist paramilitaries. There is a new police service and a Northern Ireland Assembly sits in Stormont. We have peace.

Segregation exists in neighborhoods divided by security barriers. There are over 80 of these "peace walls" in Belfast alone. Suburbs and towns are known as "nationalist" or "unionist" by their dominant population. The scabs are thin and wounds are exposed with minimal provocation. This is true.

The courage of individuals have informed many poems in this section of my book. Our hope is many more will recognize that peace has come and will work to heal the wounds, to speak truth, or to listen in silence, as did Job's friends. Let's commit to walk the roads together in prayer bringing down the security barriers and opening up the window in the wall of our hearts.

Prayer walks can replace Civil Rights and Orange marches. The unity of believers loving God and loving the neighbor as ourselves may just transform the world as Patrick transformed Ireland, and Columba changed the world, 1600 years ago.

ARMAGH

She leaned forward — looking sideways
Surveying the length of the room
And forced her speech pouring out in vowels,
Wails and howls in banshee pitch
Landing on cupped ears, tugging at grappled hearts.
Overflowing tears
Puddling
On unconcerned carpet.

Down Armagh[1] streets, over the commons
Marched the last Saturday in August
A parade of heft and chatter
A Loyal Order witness,

---

[1] Armagh is the main town center of one of Northern Ireland's counties where
the official Orange marches started in 1795. The march commemorates
William of Orange's victory over James II at the Battle of the Boyne in 1690.

Retreading history — measuring faith
Balancing trumpetries on tiptoes
Weaving a cadence of drums,
Donning orange dreams.

Her pain recharged
With every uttered syllable
Replaying charred memories,
Swollen years with stolen yesterdays
Under mounds of accumulating grief.

As loft and pride
Hoist their chins,
Searching for storm clouds,
Wrap their spite
In wafting fears of hate and fight,
Discounting green as barking dogs.

Ten years of entreating echoes
Accompany two centuries of drums and guns,
Watched over and wondered at,
By two ogling Patricks of Armagh
Cast in a concrete silence
Being Ebal and Gerizim[2],
Reminding the people of blessings and curses.

---

[2] Ebal and Gerizim were mountains adjacent to each other in Samaria, that God had Moses and his people use, to sing blessings and cursings antiphonally across to one another.

Fifers bow to bells
Tolling in a cogent flurry for Sunday worship,
As God asks
Can even one more sift of violence
Add grace to death
Already offered for life,
In my gaveled righteousness
In a Lamb's blood
Clotting your fears, shearing the tears,
Making lotus eaters[3] of fasting warlords
Who give their colors back to God, again.

---

[3] Lotus was a legendary fruit that was thought to make one peaceful and restful after eating.

THE CAT BLACK

Whispering Belfast
Wafting suspicions.
The black cat in hush
Walking the walls
Head-down silent
Tail in a sway

Cat black squats down to see
Swept up broken bricks
Meeting water canon wash
Sneaks down no sound in sight
Leaking dreams of what might be.
Purring, meandering, examining for a break
Formerly blackness, now basking in light.

On a slow crawl towards Bethlehem.
Peace is coming
Peace has come.

VIOLENCE

Lord, on the day the innocents died,
We rail and yet ache
For the insane terrorist — all of them.
I can't believe You not only created him,
But branded infinite worth
And a touch of redemptive gifting for him
Made in God's image, to help others?
What went wrong!
How can You claim him as your human?

Yes, we do recognize the motivation but,
Through your grace not the act,
The loss of his group, nation, people or religion,
Drowned in a systematic riptide of death,
Gunship helicopters
Versus their cold, round,
Smooth Davidic stones,
Swallowing up family, faith, breath and life.
Maybe even genocide
In this century of extinctions.

Is holding on to this title of defender, justified,
When innocents are selected sacrifices?
Their emotion has left and run,
Shell of once human,
Their life has been extinguished

And they are walking death.
Though they peck away at their Symbolic Satans
With detonator caps
Glued and squeezed between their blood let fingers,
God, You are not on any side
Of power-pouring and death-inviting violence.

But born to die for us
Showing life endless, graphic and creative,
You are not rumored to be
But concretely evident and present
Pleading in whistles of Spirit air,
Tears, and kingly regard,
Searching the arrogant prodigal,
Waiting for a return of this herd
Of runaways —

You have chosen us, steer riders
To herd the world
Back to life, everywhere,
In peaceful shalom
With You God
Carrying the feed of life.

PERSEVERANCE

God Most High,
The One True Blessing
The Fount of Bottomless Good
The Only Safe One who wed us as a people,
The Sure One who wears our ring of untarnished troth,
Carries us past multiple human disasters
Like toddlers through a fire
In your caress beyond tempest touch
Until death do we see.

We are your compassionate ones,
Yet sneaking increasing degrees of recognition.
Your volunteer faithful, who love salvation
Advertised and work under
Our pre-designed letterhead;
Your talent fold, who preach
By trilling resounding vowels
Tossed against the heights of heaven,
We remain stubbornly shoeless, taking steps
Towards the manifold directions of charity and want.

We carry through your Spirit's allotment,
The fruits of health and worth
But, even in your presence, our love wanes,
The apple browns and peace crumbles,

Like a dried up, stayed-out late cake
For which we sometimes, lose our taste.

You tell us not to become weary in doing good
For the forgotten and remembered,
For the poor and the rich,
For at the proper time
We will reap a harvest, if we do not now give up;
We wish to persevere past the nightfall, with You
To know the embrace of the Daylight One.
The Light of the World.

Ask us again, Maker of Moments.
Call to us one more time,
To dress for your redeeming wonder
To put on those tap dancing shoes
Made to coil in meaningful lengths
And walk us among waiting needs.
To be Still Waters for furrowed brows
Cure for those wounds of division and distrust.

Until perfection dawns, captured in your sunrise
When errors will be lost forever,
In the rough, way out there.
When we put on the robes of a lasting talk
A perfect walk, when Jesus comes.

Northern Ireland

How are we doing, Lord?
Are we incense for the gospel of God
Offering peace with every forlorn,
Impoverished minute,
Or are we steeped in professional sports
With an always changing score
And another winner to idolize tomorrow?

Do we grow global connections, threads and avenues
That help to soothe the aching bellies
Of those consuming mud pies for evening meals,
Or have we omitted and avoided distress
Like the welfare of Afghani children,
One winter dying in sub zero remote locations.
Have we prayed Isaiah 53's jailbreak verses
For all those mentally and emotionally
Carting around burdens that scale mountains,
Rounding their shoulders involuntarily,
Or, do we plead the desperate requests of others,
Including yours, Lord,
Only in formalized repetitions with marching prayers
Warming them over on our emotional stovetops
Cueing them up, penciling them in,
On long lists
With our neighbor at the end

Right before God
With his will for the world
In his overflowing arms,
Still waiting for an invitation
To be heard by his people.

The Israel of Jeremiah bragged,
God cannot run his chosen into the dust.
No harm will come to us,
Our God forgives and forgets.
We will never see the sword nor famine
For sending You on holiday.
For You own them.
And they did.
Lord, after paring down Israel for her pride,
And for bathing in earthenware idols,
You gracefully ended Jeremiah's call
With a new covenant-dressing in promises of
"To build and to plant."

Burning Coals

With the same ardor and flame,
Your servant Paul chants why to Love,
In Romans, if your enemy is hungry, feed him,
Even let him swim in desserts,
And if he is thirsty, give him something to drink,
Even your coveted Perrier water, for in doing so,
You will heap, or stack up high, and elevate, the Savior,
Distributing burning coals,
On the brows of halting breath.

The man who hates will choke on our goodness,
Embarrassed on his being admiringly present,
Melt and mend in love's cauldron,
God in the soup, and communion in our hands
And the blood still flowing,
Remaining warm, living and inside us.

Allow us God to meet your blessing
To be God's glee, to bring You glory
To grow in grace and love through Jesus,
In our walk everywhere
In step and within reach
Of your directing Holy Spirit.

Spread your people out
Serve your lasting good taste
In strands of breaching hope
On embittered despairing souls
Dressed in humanity
Scarred by suffering.
To rekindle faith by love.

DIVISIONS AND HATRED

You want us to do what, Great God?
Holding our breath for as long as possible,
No slips of soiled air,
From a bevy of kicks and punches.
In a ring of fractured humanity,
Representing nation states called the world.
Sounds more like a Ripley's "Don't believe it"
Than a pat on the back, slap on the arm
Healing and helping for broken human lives.

On second thought
Our total silence with an attentive nod,
Might gain understanding, a second chance and
Grace and peace for feverish, truant lives.
Letting the distressed fly their invectives
And sail their curses right out there;
Won't be love but we forgot that spelling lives ago.
We'll re-start and do your teaching,
Redemption of everything and everyone
Until death do we live,
As God is our guide,
With His Cloud by day and Fire at night.

This "fractured lives" is the hardest part to carry.
Everyone will have to walk home,
Carrying their burdens,
Loosing those vengeances at cold water fountains,
Not aiming them for travel like hell bombs —
No more throwing up harboring hate
Or drinking down life scars.
Anger will be burned up
Into ashes of forgotten hatreds and articles of war.
Christ has tolled the liberty bell
The pre-eminence of everything and everyone
Gifting us life in streaks of joy
And wands of jubilation.
Crippling our sadness, causing our breath.

We'll teach them to dance, God,
And lounge in your truth and love,
Vision will be accurate
Hearing will produce the elusive smile,
The distance between thought and action will narrow,
Our God will sigh content
As a reconciled affection.

Lord, are we too uptown, urban to dream Shalom?
Can we really ask You for this Peace?

Blessing

May the God of vision
Point his way
The means and the mission,
For this church
In serving the Almighty,
Here, there, and most of all,
Wherever.

GENOCIDE

God
The creation is your art work.
Spoken into being
When life burst with blessing
Hallelujahing our Maker.

The storm of sin has battered our humanity
Burgeoning strife, killing peace,
Until your coming in the earthen graze of Christ
Restored us to servant leaders and life celebrants,
To count on our lives lasting forever with You.

How will we participate against the Sudanese genocide
Inflicted in the Darfur region of their country?
All strangers
Speaking our language or not,
Having different shades of color, or not,
Recognizing Christ as God, or not,
Still have ultimate value being made in God's image,
And recommend our deepest truth and greatest love.

Was Bono of the U2 music group doing a PR stunt
When he asked our president
To commit 1% of the U.S. budget
To feed the poor of the world?

Before our trillion dollar debt,
It is not a time, like Jeremiah,
To root up and tear down,
Destroy and overthrow,
But — to build and to plant.
Hear our prayer, Lord,
And send us weighty warriors
With your cogent call of shalom.

Help us spread your peace, dear God,
Before we earn your judgment.
Please turn your ear to the pleas
Of the congregation this morning,
And may your will be done, joyfully, thoroughly
And flooded in your Grace.

LANDMINES

Planted
For dismemberment
Hidden for impact
Surprise.
But no cake and ice cream.

Watch where you step
Angels offer their lives
Clearing warfare's landmines.

HEATHER STREET

Blitzkrieg[4]
Anytime, everywhere
Pounding
1941
Serving terror in shells of grief
None ending life on
Heather Street.

Student voices
Huddled, clinging
In the coal hole
Shouting at God for a future.

Released from a plane
Circling like the eagle
Kite in sail
Ushering death
Beast of a bomb.

Cursed by a man
Scraping skinned knees
Pointing down the street
Urging God to exhale.

[4] The church we served, Crumlin Road Presbyterian, was burned to the ground in the blitzkrieg of April 1941. An elderly pensioner whom we visited lived nearby and told me this story of a man who fell to his knees in the street to pray. The bombs floated past.

Prayer answered
Bomb blasted
All feasted
Some fasted,
Out for lunch
At the funeral home
Down Heather Street.

PEACE CAROLERS

The world is your creation, God,
Where life was to grow
And giving thanks was to be our hello.
The storm of sin has battered our humanity,
We are crippled in the contortion
Of finding our own way;
But your hand, in the graze of Jesus the Shepherd,
Has restored us to peace carolers and love makers,
Adding howls and wails
from the bagpipes of hope.

Good God,
Part the current waters of strife,
As You have directly caused
In many bloodless changes of power
It is so easy to war
As leaders demonize leaders,
Sending You on vacation
Remind us humanity once more,
We are made in your image,
A common caring
A likeness of You,
Stamped and sealed in us.

Show us all pictures of the children
To tilt the killing game
Remind us to feed the left out
Till our pockets lighten
Our gait straightens
Your glory heightens
Your love parks alongside us
And our ears hear the song of Christ
At all times, and in harmony everywhere.

NOT ME

The bugle sounds.
A carousel of star minded young
Offer songs to heroes
Squealing on safe, pretend, wooden horses
Circling smiles in vocal oneness.
Until my cloud
Burst.

For I seemed to see with final eyes
A relaxed thumb,
A cold communion of index skin
And the trigger it courted.

I sweat to hold back time
But space lied
And the anger of steel speed,
Coughed
Fleeting a pungent, anonymous greeting,
A surprise
For my waiting wall
Crumbling.

I felt the rush of heat
Sear and scar in entry
Issuing its verdict
Spiraling guilty

With a gaveling crack,
Chiseling alive bone dead
Churning frantic for an exit
Dancing my life away.

Convulsing
With every frenzied query
Son of America
Stone pale
On a still pond of red
Beneath the confetti blue
Until I cried no more.

No vigil near to thank a hero's name.
All face home, sipping dreams of an armistice
Choking on a safe, safe song.
When will the bugle breach,
Beckoning howls and peals for life and peace
And passing over hails to the chief.[5]

---

[5] "Hail to the Chief" is the march played for the American president, when he appears to address the American public.

DRAGON

Sitting seraphs
Panting, waiting
Char uninvited armor

CACTUS

Fleshy stems   of prickly venom

Standing strong   and spiny, bearing no leaves

Budding a flower   but no one there to see
no one dare to touch
left to love — itself.[6]

---

[6] Individualism grew out of the French Enlightenment and affects Western civilization. "I don't need no help" is a common thought. Humanity suffers from this viewpoint.

GOOD GOVERNANCE

Governing God, we pray for your world.
You call us to ventures
Of which we cannot see the ending,
By paths as yet untrodden,
Through perils still waiting,
We ask for peace in the Middle East.

Give us faith to be pushed out, with courage
To be pulled along in perseverance,
Not knowing the where and whom of your draw,
But only that your staff and life has included us
And your love supports
The soles of our heels,
The pulse of our temples —
We live to regale You in glory,
O Wellspring of life!

Allow us to honor You
By using us
As your salutary presence
In the eye center of life storms.
We pray for peaceful change and governance
In the upheavals of Russia and Pakistan,
And for the still ground,
And no earthquakes of harmful size
In Mexico and Japan.

You are the One who cares
For this world in despair;
May we share in redeeming the time
And signing it Christ.

Robert Frost

Good fences make good neighbors,
Of what was Robert Frost trying to convince us,
That we can wave and celebrate
On Independence Day?

Two neighbors meet once a year
And walk the line to register
A guarded peace
Through an exact survey of land
And an agreement on rewalling the fallen rocks,
All in a stilted, swollen solitude.

Are we sealing ourselves in, or our neighbor out
Within this certain boundary?
Building walls too tall
Locked in solitude, quiet and alone,
Cursed confinement

If citizenship is to do good for a country —
For that walled-in neighbor,
Can we subscribe to a global patriotism,
Preserving freedoms
Raising the glow of good health,
Promoting the general welfare,
Loosing and liberating all peasant farmers?

Why do we halt our surveying at the nation's doorstep,
Is the nation state any more sacred than the continent?
Is our only flag Christ, or not?
When God and country differ,
Whom do we bow to?
Can both exist together in a peace laden love affair?

Yes, Lord, if our circle of government
Ordained, heralded, and created by You,
Rests in the flourishing quadrant, devoid of tares,
And doing your political will,
Aboard gustoes of grace
And love for our disarmed wall walkers
Wielding celebrations of You, and your Kingdom
Whom we know and where we live,
Whose reaper is Messiah
And scythe — the call of God
Garnishing souls forever more.

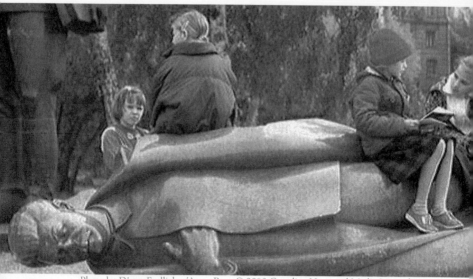

STALIN

Toppled in Moscow Park
Burnished steel forgotten flesh

Sleeping on his side kindergarten knees use him
for a lunch time drum
as they tag and seek
around the grassy mooring
sit and sing on his drydock stillness
raising voices of genocide
all called grandpa.

Once a fire   now a wick with curls of smoke
Blessed only   by passing dogs who smell,
                     bow and dispatch
                     ignoring entreaties
                     to arrest, try and shoot
                     darting off — no necks in leash
                     panting their pardons pack in liberty.

Birds land   promenade on his bare neck torso
                     cooing freedom
                     atop rusting apparel.

What once was
What used to be a fever in armor — polished might
                     dressed in a litany
                     of fitful, echoing credos
With   a hammer for hands
                     pounding innocent grain
                     purging helpless chaff
                     scythe in arms, fingering throats
                     of pausing breath counted
                     our each remaining thought for us.
Hard we swallow with naked genuflections
                     and tolling heartbeats.

Kulak arms	collect government grain
	as peasant blood washes down
	already clean cobblestone streets
	meandering along knocking
	at ten million sealed doorways.

Now fell	life lunches on evil's gullet
	dropping crumbs
	that death can't swallow
	that evil won't eat;
	knee socks eat crackers and cheese
	in silent gala
	homing safe
	in freedom's silent night.
The children	leave scraps of cling wrap plastic,
	that rusted scythes can't course.

| The school bell | tolls as the children chorus |
| | "ashes, ashes, they all fall down." |

PRAYERS
FOR THE WORLD

PRAYERS

While I was an intern and pastor's assistant during my theological training, I welcomed the task of bringing a fresh prayer during the worship service in a place in the liturgy called "Prayer for the World." I continued this practice when we moved to Belfast and worked here in a local church.

The practice evolved into a Call to Worship as time went by and sometimes was written as a Benediction for closing the worship time. The Call to Worship is a corporate call to the people who compose the local body of Christ. The Benediction is a blessing from Jesus Christ to the people through the vehicle of the speaker.

Some of these prayers are written for seasons of the church year like Christmas, Nativity, the Resurrection and Pentecost. Others are written on behalf of people-groups or situations.

Through the years I would pick and choose various parts and combine them with the events of the week or what grabbed my heart. What follows in this section are the latest versions of these prayers.

It has been said that what God has to say to us is more important than what we say to God. Please let these prayers invite that holy silence whereby the still small voice of the Almighty will speak loudly to your soul and cause you to follow Him.

FAITH AND PRACTICE

Blessed be your holy, loving ways, dear Lord,
All life is straightened and smoothed out by You,
Made Spirit rich, mistakeless and complete,
Like a mason mending a broken wall,
Grouting until the crack is gone.

You are patient in revisiting your returning answers
For our fresh, same queries.
Your clarity remains our question,
Your practice remains our theory,
Your love is our taste but never do we swallow,
Our faith needs your filling.

What about the world, apart from us?
Can the broken and repaired hose bib
Quench the thirst of a parched universe?
Who is whole enough to govern
And serve the rest of us?
Can we adequately paint in your image,
Swab the canvass of the creation,
With the brushstrokes of redeemed living,
That You breathe and be,
Doing all things with an abundance,
Of compassion, mercy and justice?

We can swallow, "It be we, Lord."
Cover our incomplete gestures of love
With yours, fresh every day,
Like a final exam, a smooth righteousness
"Always passing," because of You, Christ.
You have touched your toe, on redeemed earth.

Give us your work to do,
Running slower and not far behind,
While You greet returning prodigals who,
Begin to celebrate your Peace on earth,
Your advent beckon
Your warmth and way
Of a present, eternal life,
A canvass of hope
A God of grace,
A holy point; a Christ forever,
With your people,
Sealing the cracks of the creation.

PERSONAL GOD

When we pray for your World,
There's so much involved
And so many
To count.
Finger quick soldiers erase millions
Of objecting image bearers.

Our eyes blink in wishing not
And tear with regret.
Over a mobile display of wartime technology
On parade, above the soil.

Did America close your ears of compassion,
Jibing a "just war"
Then glorying in their take charge,
First strike capability?

Lord God, You know all seven billion people.
We're all delicately woven in your image —
Have worth, cradle life,
Some calling You,
Most praying to any god who they idolatrously imagine,
Wearying that their children need food,
They need shoes,
Clothing, health, meaning, a friend and a family.

Thank You God for shouting reminders,
In the book of James.

How do You cater and hand out your love to us all
Wandering and marauding sheep
In your pen fold called the World,
Who, would rather eat each other,
Than share your blessing,
On a set schedule of history
At war tables of death and misery?

You are the only, Personal Being
In and beyond this universe,
Who only does what You say You will.
You are Trust and Promise,
Will and Word,
Whose theory and practice
Always equal justice and mercy,

Who exudes love and serves care.
You multiply Wisdom.
Your thinking, even your ways,
Clear the paths with mystical certainty.
Your wealth has no decimal places
Like the barns of Oprah and Turner,
Murdoch and Gates.

Who You are finds our needs;
You chased down the excommunicated
Man Born Blind,
Assuring him You would not and could not spell
Orphan or left alone
Relationships is your created lasso and,
Just power in governance
Makes your total Trinity,
Delighted and dancing.

May we not miss your Invitational;
We don't need You crying over Jerusalem again, Jesus
Saying You would have gathered us as children
If Ulster and America had been willing;

Take all of us for your wholesome purposes.
Grant us prayerful arms to hold on during your ride.
Have mercy on your world in sin
And seed the fruitful, bearing and parenting
Love, Justice, Compassion and Truth,
To gain ground on
Those iron horses of annihilation.

Forgive any leaders who know your name,
Love your wealth, twist and rewrite history,
Even your Gospel,
But are too busy
To learn the You beyond the forgiving breath.

Use us God, to keep up your reputation.
Grant us life.
Make us authentic
Keep us vulnerable.
We want to change your world
Sweeping up and away
One piece of broken life at a time,
Offering one cup of rest, for all time.
We love You, God
Who offers open arms
To a swollen and beaten humanity.
May we touch the healing
And know our God is Jesus the Christ.

Thank You for the call,
May we return to You, love, worship and glory.

COMMUNION

Jesus, Giver of our every breath
Leash, for wandering appetites,
Temper of our tearful regrets,
This day
With deepest shalom,
Give us the Bread of Heaven.

Merciful One,
May our offered lives be enough
To move people
Towards your waiting comfort,
To spread many more
Chances of forgiveness.

At humanity's mealtime,
Correct vision
Soften scoff
Burgeon praise.
Alight the storm clouds of your Glory,
Changing the face of sin
You call, we care
True God
We worship.

Just One, seed the crop of your blessed rule;
Your prophets are sleeping
On moneyed mattresses of
Personal peace and hollow core images
With no public stir
From the salt and light.

Are we so bereft of talking justly
That You use someone else
Who doesn't even know You,
Contributing more questions
Than our ordained ministers,
In dogging justice
With fuelled orations
Holding a video recorder
Donning a baseball cap?

Teach us all to shout, sing, and dance
To your liberty bell,
Christ Almighty,
Christ alone,
Christ Divine!

Holy God, tip your bottomless cruet
Of exceeding grace
In waterfalling fullness on us,
Flowing down for sips of wholeness
At Communion's hoedown;
Tripping with the Master
On life's nourishing dance floor,
Revolution feeding revolution.
In your time
We will sit, celebrate
And feast on life.

CHRISTMAS

Manger King
Swaddling royal
Time starting over —
Rewinds its clock.

Life teething on
Manger meditations
Ponders a fresh forgiveness
Unblemished by sin.

Choirs once stranded at Eden's gate
Now spiral out in downpours of praise
Drinking in full cups of joy.

A fresh start everywhere
When every stem becomes a flower,
Every voice pierces the dark, and
God gets cradled by all, calling

O Sovereign Monarch
On incarnational stealth
Christ the King.

NATIVITY

We know all about parachute rides, Lord.
Shot from an airplane,
Skydivers fall like a kite in sail
Nervously eyeing distance downward.
Waiting for the chute to spread its sheet,
To catch air
And smoothly sail us to land safely,
Kissing the earth.

Your penetration at Bethlehem was celebrated
in a whisper, on incarnational stealth.
You snuck in as the infant King
Not wishing to disturb the sinful ions, yet,
That You would later obliterate,
Blowing them apart by your disintegrating —
Perfect living.
Where's the regalia and sovereignty in that?

Your sent-out ones also greeted your coming,
As the Messiah who would line up straightness.
How could You as the coronational God,
Fresh from Trinity bliss,
Purposely sidestep the parade,
We wanted to force on You
The crown, the throne that
We stained, sanded, and guarded;

Whether the paint matched your staff
of love and mercy, or not;
You chose an ornery donkey instead,
shuffling down a winding, dusty road
To drink your justice, that will
Straighten every curl on bent heads.

Lord, in your world,
Convict us to use Power, Money and Wisdom
In creative, changing ways
Of Truth and Might, within limits;
With money drenched in a compassionate value
Counted by folded, praying hands,
With Wisdom, residing in You, Lord
And given to us as a gift we need,
Choking our pride on the plain drink tea of humility.

We cheer this first act, Lord,
In your sheepfold of grace.
We look for the continuance of Creation
In your coming transit of glory
In the sky on way to earth
Wearing footsteps as King,
Standing in a recreated earthen vista
Before and with the gird of truth
And the God who loves us.

THE WHOLENESS OF GOD

Sinless God, Holy God
Who not only made rules
But kept them joyfully
Bearing the character of Law
As the person of Christ,
The diploma of grace,
For us, human,
Needing repair and restoral.

You are the expression of everlasting wholeness.
The cure for every bruised particular
Within the broken creation,
Holding the explanation of the sand grain.

Bordering the mystery of the snow capped land mass
In acres of sky.
Understanding the simple and profound child.
Following the circular thought of an Einstein.

You are language for the intangibles
The richness of concern,
Wealth for all compassion
Glory topping goodness,
You are God.

You are the unblemished lamb
The song of perfection
The trumpet of salvation
The God who touches the world
Who yanks on our hearts, all the way down and deep
To cause us to grace this universe,
With daily spoonfuls of love, life and meaning.

THE RESURRECTION

Risen Holy God,
It feels like an apocalypse down here
At these war and worst-times;
Grant us courage and fidelity
To sing your love
And be your sheep,
Tooting Easter horns in restless meadows;
Touting peace with torpedo accuracy.

Let us accept God's blessing
Sealed in gift wrap —
Precious gift
Resurrection
Waged for You
Carried now contained inside You.

Who are You, O next in line
Will You feed your lengthening prodigal famine?
Flood your thirst
Break the proud fast?
God waits.   God ponders.
God beckons.

Lord, You do not call us to die for the world,
Your death is enough to capture all, as innocent;
But over high hurdles and before convulsing wealth,
We are charged to show different attitudes,
Like compassion, grace,
Life as hearing aids for those we love
And those we struggle, with hating.
Let us live for You and with You
O Certain and Close God,
Mimicking your life
Poised with good news
Peculiar and poignant
Authentic and ardent.

And God, don't forget errant nations,
Drowning in the swamp of violence
And horrific hate.
Unleash your chorusing faithful.
Place us
Awkward, bundled with telling tears
As heralds of joy;
We will do it. We will serve, O Lord.

Looking upon the death, giving palettes for living rest,
Shelling them with ensuing mercy
Standing them up as targets for peace
Let them hear our voiced oneness shaping justice,

Offering a corralling compassion,
Touching them with a love that burns,
lights up, and fires — faith.

And may these fruits of the Spirit
Hang like sugared marbles
On their clustered vines,
Growing them a vineyard of life.

As we examine the lost body this day
From the remainder grave clothes —
People, Jesus is in the air
Alive and inviting,
Near, and willing to forgive.
Christ has risen!

The Lord bless you and keep you
The Lord be kind and gracious to you
The Lord call you to redeem the culture,
Redo the world,
And give you Joy and Grace in His dance with you,
Strolling hand in hand,
Talking heart to heart with God.

PENTECOST

Great God of us all
Curtail prejudice from the breathing mouthfuls
Of our covetous exhale.
We know it lodged in us all after the beginning.
Yet, may we know now, a little bit,
From your redemptive scurry,
The scent, service and cure of your holy speech,
Steeped in mercy.

Remind us over and over, more and again,
Seventy times seven,
That we are all people of your call,
Not "in spite of" our ethnic hue,
But because we are black and red, white and yellow,
And all purposeful shades in between.
This is your Spirit's paint brush,
For the gleam and color of your creation,
And we are all aboard, being made,
Tinted, and reconciled
In your loving, rainbow image.

Don't stop there God!
Purpose and beckon that we live together,
Adopt Unity as our family name,
Give up our Cainish killing,

Recommending your gracious ocean of gospel
Offered to all and each,
Embraced and secured
By us ever-praising, God-lifting, lovers of Christ,
On earth as it is in heaven.

We chant hope in the noose of distress
And unscheduled war,
Sickness and uninvited loss in our lives,
For it is by You, we breathe, and for You, we endure
Washing friendship, in your sustaining pools
Of relieving grace
On this earthen tarmac of break and fracture
For the shine of your glory, God Present and Personal.

Till that future time at the ascent of history's curtain
When the sun will rise at daystart,
Hesitate above, and will not go down,
As You coronationally land, our face to face Christ,
Light for us,
And we hallelujah You,
With Pentecosted verse,
As your grateful, revering people,
Wearing color tones from a donor God.

GOOD GOD

As your people, You call us to help
You call us to ventures
Of which we can see only to the turn
And initially, never know what's beyond,
On paths circuitous and troubling,
Through perils unsettling.

Give us the faith of ambassadors
To be pushed out and pulled in by You,
To be shaped by your warming potter hands.
Allow us to honor You more
Moved by your loving us more
Use us in your world
To exercise redemption
To offer your wellspring
To cradle justice and captain mercy
On the lawless sand grains of the worn-down earth.

Revive Good God
Give us your rest
So that people may know, who You are
And who we may be and love You for it
Tending Shepherd, Sovereign Ruler, Resolute God.

MISSION

O Lord,
We only know this life of who we are
By your provisional serve of purpose and meaning,
Your pin point at the which way of things.
Your revelation
The Word of God.

Grant that the causeway of faith
Through your gifting Holy Spirit
Will align and regiment our hearts
For your daily illumination and shuffle of blessing.

Forgive us our overlooks, rain on our disregard
Spell it all clear, show us your glory.
Cause our feet to mimic your walk,
Poised with good news
Purposed with redemptive fire.

Support us all the days long
In all the endeavors we breathe for You —
Until the shadows lengthen
And our gait is no longer rhythmic,
And the evening comes
And the busy world is hushed,
The fever of life is over,
And our work is done.

Then, in your mercy
Claiming us with your signature grace
Hand us foot to foot and face to face
As cloudy witnesses have climbed before,
To your guarded and glorious promise of
Living with You, forever,
O Lover of our souls and Light to the world,
God out there, God always
God in us, God only.

WHO'S THE GREATEST

Omnipotent Christ
Help us help You
Care for the children
In this lifetime, above the ground.

Loose their laughter, flow their tears like a sedative
Sleeping war, stilling violence
Imparting giggles of blasting innocence,
Elevating life to shining redeemed levels
Of truce in neighboring, world sandboxes
Protesting their own savage dying
Sighted in too many adult crosshairs
Recognizing only shadows and stopping their age.

Don't let nations swirl in preoccupation over
"Who's the greatest,"
Making idols, grabbing your essence, Lord
That we fail to hear their voices in song
Or fail to see with their eyes
Of no grid, no agenda reality
Of fun and games, truth and love.

This day, your day, God
Wheel them safely around injury,
Far from the clutch and choke of illnesses
Free from the butt end of injustice,

To grow up in Christ
Everywhere in the world
Digging in the dirt of a peaceful back yard
Playing hours of hosted games on front-yard concrete
Welcoming the approval of your applauding Trinity,

Caressed in the long arms of God — announcing
"Whoever welcomes this little child
In my name
Welcomes me.
And whoever welcomes me,
Welcomes the One who sent me.
For he who is least among you all —
He is the greatest."

SPORTS IDOL

Things happen so fast, Lord;
Technology doesn't have to ring the doorbell,
Like everybody else, to talk to us.
It dances through the phone block
Meeting sleepy, unprepared ears.
Ready to anoint us
With the latest reports on popular culture.

But You, dear Lord, hold our hearts,
You want our lives more than
Formally spewed confessions.
How can You compete, Lord,
Along with the lure of these athletic gladiators,
With the grip of highly entertaining recreational sport
Before our eyes, in our ears, and on our laps?
Do we dare even to "pencil You in?"

We do not, and defer to squeezing You out,
Within our manageable, small portions
of prayer and worship.
Warning: God is on the gridiron today
Rooting for no particular team.
Teach us, Holy One,
How to address your concerns, for us, and others,
In a world that You loved to death, and raised to life,

Sprinkling your cultural values
On those bearing your image,
Touching every living country You know so well,
Let us strain to hear your accented
Syllables of life over our palpitating hearts;
Pour silken draped certainty,
On the taste buds of our wandering thoughts.

Let us hear the God of it all,
Tag our distracted hearts,
Shooting with stuck arrows of love and courage,
Breeding charity, care and compassion, on us,
Each of us having a person in mind
Every one, the world in interest.
Let us love in the relationship You give us.
In a whirlwind of spiritual activity
By offering You glory, our silence,
Opening our attention,
Listening for your words on our thoughts,
For sixty seconds of speechless unity
Feeding on the Christ of God
Waiting for your entrance
Hearing your speech.

GOD'S WORLD

For your world, God,
Who is ever climbing out of your boat of rest,
Dog paddling away for invisible shores.

For your world,
Carved outside, in ardent bloom
Inside, with your gifted image
For each of us.

For the world
Of waste, discard and violence
Discouraging the purposes You created for us,
To sing and shout hallelujahs over —

For the lost ones, Lord,
Everywhere
In a seven billion peopled crowded earth
Of elbows needing wings —

Use us who yearn for justice, and your glory;
Save, dear God, and we will know
It was your heaven scent, again —

Once more,
Your walk on water
Your birth on earth
Your love and breath.

The well spring of life —
For your world, Lord.

SET ASIDE

Eternal God, our side by side hope,
And lover of our lives,
Our always help in times of trouble:
Forgive us for seeing You
As someone to set aside
As the Sovereign to address at only time of
Dead-ends, distress and wars
Instead of the God to adore in Glory.

Show nations and continue to show nations
Ways to work out differences,
Encourage us adding Mediator to the winding praise,
Of how we know You.
Don't let threats multiply in your world.
Make all changes of power bloodless and sleep full
Mimicking your past, holy manipulations
In Russia, the Philippines and Liberia,
And for tribal peace in Kenya.

Let us be gospel in the dents and cracks of life.
Show us how to use power
That builds and empowers lives
More than destroys.

Let us relearn the spelling of compassion
Let us rehear the God of justice,
Let us return to our relationship with You, O Lord,
With a master plan of peace in our arms
And fortified with your garrison of hope
In the midst of stillborn artillery
And an absence of smoking weaponry.
In every country, we pray this, Loving God,
But especially in our own.

THE TIGER

Dear Lord,
The world is out of control again.
We have been the caretakers
Of your creation from the beginning.
We need help with this dragon,
Santa Ana winds
Breathing arson fire.

Lord, fire is like the tiger,
It kills without a collar.
Its power is sinister, in destruction,
A warmth and health
Life and breath,
When it remains in bounds.

Watching fire charred living space,
We have nightmares of Hell,
3,000 degrees of judgment
Twisting pylons, swallowing homes
With people desperately defending their memories
Holding Ace Hardware hose nozzles,
In a fleeting retreat
Coughing agony.

God, now
Help us take care of all your image bearers
The needing humanity, the frail fraternity,
You are the Waters of Blessing,
The Riptide of Care
We're in love with your goodness.
You're the Shoreline for every storming wave,
The Final Port
For calling home good and cursing the evil.

You make us glad for living and joyful in song
Even, breathing smoke, tasting the heat,
And swallowing ash;
You honor us with carrying life
Calling us daughters and sons, wrapped in family
Blessed with grace, content with pitchers
Of quenching peace.

Dying once, we tear
Eternally yours, we sing
Out of our bounty of hallelujah heartbeats,
Offering song for our rebuilding, bent-straightening
Redeemer Savior
The Hopeful Rain for lives in fire and thick smoke,
The Cold Water place for every soul,
With him who extinguished the power of death,

The Living Shower for longing life.
God alive
God always
Trinity of grace and glory,
Haven of Rest.

BENEDICTION

God send us out, this day
To needy places
With needing people,
To water down the fires in their hearts,
In the name of the Father,
Son and Holy Spirit
Amen.

WORLD

Lord, we turn away our minds
In a frozen fear
From pictures of cinder blocks
Gracing the air
Sailing in slow motion,
Not building houses —
Crushing Israeli skulls
In passing automobiles,
Devoid of guns to kill cleanly.

"Healer of All Nations"
Help your people
Urge Northern Ireland who cares for You
And America who cares for the Moon and Mars
To be injected with the reality that
Both Israelis and Palestinians
Maybe not knowing, are still —
Made in your image — human
And worth living with
As well as dying, God,
That is what You told us, and they are those
As well as us, You died for.
Help us help them, God

And remind us, locally, to conduct our own church
With holy Truth and far-deep Love,
Behind your march, and
Never as a tennis match

With hard services to score a point
Hitting angry aces skipping past peopled end-lines
Massing solo baseline returns, doing it my way
And soft, unexpected lobs skirting the net
Of grace and harmony,
Keeping score, disinterested and inconsequentially
Fifteen-love, thirty-love, forty-love,
What person, so what, who cares.
Let's call it Game and rather do it your way, O God,
Refreshed with Shalom and Aloha
With wholesome, whole life volleys
With shaking hands, giving hugs
Match point, as we live the love for and with each other,
Sensing the crisp endowment of unseen joy,
Recommending to the world
The reality and rule of Jesus, our Savior.
August Giver, Swab of Healing,
Guest for our Emptiness,
God for our Lives.
In Belfast, in Dublin.

BLESSING

God, send us Everywhere
Turning stones, drying tears
Sleeping war and burying fear
For Glory is your Being
And You are our Life
We belong to You
Send us, God.

GOD LISTENING GOD SPEAKING

Living as One in your multiple of Trinity
Aid for our failing hearts
Fingers for our knotted thoughts
Hearing for every distress
Sight for returning prodigals,
Savior of our soul.

Show us, how to be more than
Self committed, empty and vain,
Losing ourselves in Lone Ranger ways,
Amassing threats to take our football home,
Sporting Napoleon's pomp with our hand in our chest,
Warning to grow like the cactus,
Fleshy stems — of prickly venom
Standing strong — and spiny, bearing no leaves
Budding a flower — but no one there to see
No one dare to touch, left to love itself

Encourage us, Teaching One, to be:
Faithful in wedlock
Loyal at work
Absorbed in church
Be the body of Christ
Connected in worship
Knit in unity

Willing to pray together
Loving our neighbor, far and near
Even those cursed with error
Joined to our God
And richly bound in our relating.

You are the One who shapes goodness
Collects our wanders
A net for our stumbles
Gives sail for us windblown
And our anxious chasing breath.

God So Good
The One who never leaves us
In our pains and stirs us during the solitary times,
Who never drops an echo.
Who can fear the worst
When we go hand and hand with God
Who has counted us by our hairs
And who knows us by name,
Who loves us by his grace.

FATHERS

God help the fathers
Elevate the longing of their want,
To grow up their children to You.

To teach them to bear
Through the behemoth of brokenness,
Carrying the uplift of hope
With their pausing breath.

Make the Holy Spirit the prayer interest
Of every child in motion with God
Returning them fruit
Squeezed on swelling hearts.

And reward the searching father
With the tureen of faith,
Hopeful inspirations,
And the ladle of charity
For teaching his family to love its Lord.

And then, ask us again, Eternal Father,
Call us one more time
To dress for your redeeming alterations,
To carry joy in our shoes,
Ready to tap wherever You rush.

And walk us among waiting needs, worldwide,
Shiite, Sunni, Kurd, Israeli, Lebanese, Palestinian
Of Fathers, and Mothers, and families,
To be still waters for furrowed brows,
Cure for those wounds of division and destruction,

Until perfection dawns, captured in your sunrise
When error will be lost forever, in the rough,
way out there,
When we put on the robes of a perfect talk,
A steady walk, arm and arm in Christ
In the family of God.

High God Holy God

Shall we pray for our world,
For the seven billion people everywhere,
Stuffed in the various,
Trying pockets of redeemed life?

High God Holy God
You rule the way of peoples,
Directing us like a watercourse wherever You please.
Construct your sound wall with flood lights on
Every warring sovereign.
Work with those who search for peace
Casting bloodless votes, causing worship rest.

Place your just and merciful palms
On your peoples' shoulders
Facing us at the kernel of your will
The what and when, space and time of everything.

Rain on us your restoration,
Beckon the storms of hope,
Drench us in the flood of peace,
Give us You, God.

Enrich us Lord, mature and fulfill us
Not as a strong Samson, nor a wise Solomon, nor even
A wealthy Bill Gates,
But wrapped in the blessing and glory of Christ
Where justice resides, in a manifest shower of meaning
With whom life is topped off,
Who took the form of humanity
To bear a faithful offspring,
Forever in Him.
Forever with Him
Forever God.

HANDHOLD OF GOD

May the handhold of God
Make you generous with your life
And creative with your plenty.

Hold outs from evil
Hand outs for mercy
Becoming a song for this life
Giving glory to your Maker,
And life to your ways.

BIG TENT REVIVAL

Plan your big tent revival, God.
We will never be less ready,
But we need to swallow your holiness,
For life in the bread of heaven
And love our neighbor as our self.

Encourage us,
To offer jailbreak; freedom for all
Tasking not only the corners of our checkbooks,
But the big bucks too
Reserved for our never miss holiday.

Use our repaired hearts
Caressing your will,
Cast our hooks,
At your passing grace,
Their pausing breath.
Sounding ripples of redemption case.

Forgiveness,
Return, revival, redemption
New things
Let us do it as a dance, for You God

BENEDICTION

May the God of might and mercy,
Send you out and about
With His finger point,
To go to whom He gives you
Moved and guided
by His always Holy Spirit.

Spreading life
On the world
That you may partake
And they may know
God's life and thoughts through Him.

THE SHAPE OF GOD

Dear God
Spread your people out
And serve your lasting good taste
In strands of breaching hope
On embittered, despairing souls
Dressed in humanity
And scarred by suffering.

This world has 850 million undernourished people.
2.8 billion live on less than $2 per day.
Help us to remember them in tangible ways
With checkbook dollars for nourished stomachs
And opportune freedoms.

Let us not forget Katrina, Lord,
Enliven and rebuild side by side with them
Now, out of public eyesight,
And not wanting to be orphaned
From the rest of us.

Aid and direct us, Lord,
To have rich and considerate discussions
On 75 million dollars of American involvement
In Iranian affairs over
Their method of governance
And uranium enrichment.

Help us in pacifying Pakistan, Kenya
Afghanistan and Somalia,
At the core of Muslim life,
Avoiding and retracting insults
And blasphemy to them,
But preserving cartoon criticism and liberty's dissent.

OH GOD

Oh God of the world,
God of the creation,
Light to the hearts that see You,
Life for the souls who love You,
Strength of the thoughts that strain for You
At the desperation points in our lives.

To turn from You is to die senseless,
To turn to You is life endless
To turn with You is to dance with joy,
Caught by spiraling degrees of never wasting
Ever blessing.

To abide in You is to know the seams of your Glory,
To speak with You is to feed
On the Gifter of all there is,
You are the owner, title and deed
Of wholesome everything,
You are the surety that every good gift
comes from above.

More than human, You are the One and Only Divine
You are God.
Although we carry no credentials to your throne,
Pay no acceptance fees
Hold no free passes

Know no other human wearing perfection
To recommend us
We do come, by the fullness of just only your name
Jesus Christ, Our Savior and Redeemer
Not in expectation of wealth, wisdom, or power,
But to pray for your world, Lord,

Christians shun and avoid the sound of everything illegal,
The Mexican immigrants wear that assigned branding,
And don't they also carry the Bible's tag of "the poor"?
Do they surface again and again, with gulping breath
As the dirt oppressed on the pages of Amos,
Shrouded in sorrow and a condemned silence?

We pray for the rest of your world
That needs your full squeeze of justice and mercy,
The fertile gospel from your engaging prophets.
Move us to learn the wisdom of your peace,
Show us revel, in living shalom,
Celebrating You as the essence of tranquility,
Breaking down the walls of partition
In feuding ghettos across the globe,
Making room for the Balm of Gilead
Who will soon be seen.
The One who loves us
And whom we love.

CREATOR GOD

Almighty, Creator God,
Your spoken word at the start,
Caused the waters to seek the land
With fish that show your grace at rest.

The air to be speckled with birds
That shower the dawn with song
And dismiss its light at day set.

We take pleasure in the worth
And wealth of your creation
And will take pains to sustain its richness.
We pray for those in power
To use your provision
In limited scales
For the greatest life
For rich, and surely poor,
Including the wobbling penguin
And the silent Himalayan peak.

Honoring You limitlessly, Lord
Choosing your august life
Accepting your transforming love
God who has done marvelous things,
Setting the table of Nature

With the curl of leaf, bounding black bear,
The scented speech of a rose
And rocks that sleep
We praise You at evening tide
Carrying baritone psalms with our bass amen.
To breathe the creative
Hallelujahs.

FULL

May God in endless mercy
Carry the whole living church
To a joyful resurrection
In all things churchful,
In things all familyful,
In jobs and work bountiful
To our world all needful
By the Holy One all powerful
For the glory of God
Who loves you, endlessly.
Amen.

JEREMIAH

You're so involved with your creation, God.
You can't stop sliding off
Your heavenly throne
Stretching out — creation wide
With your limbs of mercy and justice,
With involvement on earthen ground
Where your world will be.
And where, heaven will be recreated.
At the second coming of Christ.

We hear You announcing in Jeremiah
That the prophet would experience
One of your visits
As You reached out and touched his mouth, saying
"Now I have put my words in your mouth."
Full of joy that Jeremiah was the receptor
Of your gifting presence,
Portioned out to him in audible Hebrew grammar,
Full of grief, that You directed him
To a message You served as
Uprooting and tear down, destruction and a bitter end.

His Calling Card

May the God of
Grace, Hope, and Love,
Father, Son, and Holy Spirit

Walk you around
As His calling card
To all those lifting heads,
Wanting to know
Where the joy lives.

A CUPPA

A Cuppa

In the culture of Northern Ireland, there is always time for a visitor. If a person turns up at your door they are invited in and a "cuppa" is offered, and always crowned with a biscuit. A good friend will say "May I have a biscuit" if you forget to offer one. Hospitality is shown but it takes a long time or a bit of confidence to open up and go deep.

The common phrase is "whatever you say, say nothing" and it is deadly. Fears are harbored and emotions are suppressed. Sometimes as an outsider, a "blow in" which is another phrase we've learned, you offer an ear and people tell you something profound. You then have the opportunity to feed it back to them as welcomed truth.

This section begins with two poems written for Lynda Tavakoli's writing class, in particular to Belfast. The first entitled "Linen" was written for a group reading at the Irish Linen Museum in Lisburn. The next one "Leaving Bubbles" was written for the 100th anniversary of the sinking of the RMS Titanic in 2012 and was also read during a group reading at the Irish Linen Museum. Both of these subjects have tremendous impact on the history of Northern Ireland and both are recently being redeemed.

Linen is a remarkable fabric that dates back 4000 years to Egyptian antiquity. Belfast became "linenopolis" and up until the 1970s had 28 large mills and machinery works to support these mills. Boys entered secondary school and went out to work at Mackie's and girls went to the mills.

Few discuss the loss of industry and the economy, but rather the long history of animosity as the source of The Troubles in Northern Ireland. The blame is generalized into "they" and hundreds of years of history. Rarely said is "we could have, or we didn't…" The lost art of linen weaving can be redeemed by considering the process of weaving a tapestry of relationships.

The Titanic was a source of shame for Belfast. In 2005 it was redeemed by the vision of developers to build out the vacant lands of the old industrial area. The Titanic Quarter houses film studios, a college, a hotel, and the Public Records Office of Northern Ireland (PRONI). The centerpiece of the Titanic Quarter is the state of the art Titanic visitor center designed by Eric Kuhne and Associates. It capitalizes on the RMS Titanic, which was built on the adjacent slipways, but more importantly it redeems the pride of workmanship and center of industry which was Belfast in 1912.

Our favorite part of this development which we visit weekly is The Dock Walk and the pop-up honesty Dock Café. This work was started by a small group of chaplains assigned to the area to provide respite, prayer and practical guidance.

The poems and some prayers in this section are ordered randomly. They date over several decades. *Plain Drink Tea* is a collection of thoughts and word pictures for life. My hope is they speak to you with value worth sharing over a cuppa.

Occasion poems are important because they have great consequences when interspersed with normal life. An example would be bereavement. Death is a part of life but must be noted, paused for, and marked with appropriate weight less we forget our own frailty.

LINEN

Green leaves escape flax stems
Join trembling blue buds, graduating
Before swift, admiring glances
Lounging in soft loamy soil
Dressed for moderate, inviting temperatures.

Spin and yarn from plant to finish,
Resistant to marauding carpet beetles,
While moths burrow out
Aiming for more friendly fabric.

Linen purple and fine
Becomes a durable song
An endearing life for
Believing hearts
Birthing peace
Leaving home
Bearing a sanguine hope.

LEAVING BUBBLES

A safe boat
On a fomenting sea
Maiden voyage
Crowning the ship
With imprinting nods
Of awe and wonder, on stage.

Three million soft rivets
Begin popping like champagne corks,
The ship afloat begins to drink,
Belch and chatter its broken way,
Down to waiting ground.

Only no one there to see
No one dare to touch
Left to love itself.
Drunk, foundered and full,
Pleading to a blind sky,
Aimed straight down
Leaving bubbles…

MORE THAN

Her wings are forged with steel in sleeves
Cut with aspiring liquidity
Catching eyes, arresting breath

Her move is swift, undaunted and without feet.
Weaving her solo song and distant message
In meandering flight

Being herself, beyond beauty.
Lancing any thoughts of who she could become

Her heart holds out disturbing warmth
Loosing the carnage shells of love
Making her more than angel,
Rare for the Fall
Common in God's wink and toss.

MARGARETTE

The boat that sailed, had sought the port
Only to find the gale fighting the shoreline.
Her head tilts, unsure of her sails
Staring at the bottom of the boat,
Waiting for the waves to flatten in serenity.
Briny knees in spilling teacup.

Tossed asleep awake by God before the eye blinks.
Life, beckoning across the brine
Rest is her shore
Quiet the seas
Margarette her fame.
So quietly caring
Tending the sheep to her table.
Everything to everyone
Living the goodness of her God.
Pung[7]

Her head lifted
Her eyes know the hallow of his governing arms,
He knows the hollow of her cradled frame,
Who greets heals and joys with
Margarette.

---

[7] Pung — A call of victory in Mah Jong, a Chinese game.

TOGETHER

Eyes meet
Voices soften
Recommend
A kiss.
It lands
Caring.

Will you dance with me?
Swelling dreams ride on
Tight turns
Cupped hands, courting rings
Revolution feeding revolution

Easy smiles
Enjoy each other
Effortless muse.

Words
Unfolding lives
Caught on care
Between verbs,
Pledge waiting fruit
Picked off lowered boughs.

Stems of reclining stillness
Stand up and smile
In calm and greening grasses
Shine off God's face,
Talk the world into tenderness.

STREETSHOOTER

The boy who loved the ball
Never missed the morning's shoot-around
Peppering footwork on the court's greeting green.
The pavement sank with gentle care
On way-up high bounds
For all-net jumpers.

The boy who loved the ball
Cut to imagined picks and cross-over drives
With arrogant sneaker squeals —
Brought watching ash and
The once stolid redwood
To cheers, with waving arms.

The boy who loved the ball
Pushed wind on seeming dunks,
Breeze remembering to bow and blow,
And in a playful tease
Shook the sandbox in blinding eyes.

The boy who loved the ball, one on one
As stray dog trails Streetshooter
To the basket,
Snapping at a loose ball
Barking at his elevation.
Scores two, chasing dog.

The boy who loved the ball,
The one who grew our smiles,
Bobbie, who twirled life
On one finger's eager, life tall spin
Stopped his worship and looked up to see
Who dropped the rain?

Sky sheeting with weather
Tears drop and dress pausing breath
Years of fruit and year of fallow.
As Jubilee calls a time out,
The boy who loved the ball
Became the court who loved the boy.

KIND THOUGHTS
FOR ALAINA LEE STOTHERS

"Thank you for your kind thoughts."
They more than mope in a cloud
They ring around your heart,
They march, whistle, stroll and contend
Aiming at evil's bull eye
Releasing abundant joyfuls of
Landing love.

Receiving touch
Seasoned with care, concern and life.
Resounding tolls
Of reclining rest.
Peace appearing
On this corner of buffeted earth.

EAGLE

Enthroned on spired peaks
With exacting eyes, glowing marbles
Steeping above, he scans for a deserter
Inquiring below, the still life motions
Intrigued by dusting trails and zigzag lives
The eagle dances.

Shuffling talons on swollen crags
Kite on sail, crowned with azure
Cross on breeze, measuring beneath.

Makes a confession
Before the ride on fitful prey,
Tuning his tears to
The blues of a throaty justice;

Longing to lie down with the lamb,
Catching claws in a kiss of peace.

CYNTHIA

A flower
strained in the wind
Testing its tallness
Sends petals to Santiago
To hear its poets eat metaphors
Chew on sounds of life,
Justice, mercy, liberty and love.

The flower
Arching its wings is now,
Seeking the sky harvest of bloom
Pointing to hope
Knowing its name.

INCANDESCENCE

A candlewick lit
Releasing truth in curls of smoke
Over sleeping sand
Across desert trails
Onto derelict eyes
Of pleading granules.
Picked me out, and lifted up
Knowing my number
Among sand grain miles
Uttering
Slices of certainty
Silken draped
On the thirstbuds
Of my breaking thoughts.
Incandescence.
I look above and smile
To dry their tear
I breathe to believe
In the Light I see
Down I go my voyage through
Leaving bubbles
Greeting glows of a face
I knew I know.

JEREM

Fleeting freshman
Churning like helicopter blades
Dizzying through
Deadline assignments.
While
Lacrosse shot arms
Twist, cup and unleash
Sound barrier seeds
Past crestfallen, scarecrow goalies.
Studying
History after history
Dates of tagged significance
Places of marked catastrophe.
History on history of
People with no resistances
Carpets for grand ascendancy.
Living
The ways we are
Annals of brokenness
Sending our American prayers on postcards
To a rich, stealth savior.
Walking
Jet Blue wings, turning green
Before the envy of
Rival, onlooking big birds.

Praying
Pounding heart
Wondering his way
At home with the unseen
Talking to God
Who answers his everyday's "Whasup"
With caressing embrace
Haunting regard
Total gifting love
For who this Jerem be.

ICE-SKATING

Arms of elation
Skate into fresh lime breeze
Linking in a taste of communion
Breathing out puffs of hope
Turning figure eights
Raising high hands
Of yipping praise.

Cells of jealousy
Resisting life, demanding space
Discarding peace, begin protest
Skates twist into a hardened fist of frost
Cold winds crowd the skulking grey.
A fall, a halt, a grimacing nod.

Motionless maiden.
Restless intrigue, violence beckons
A last dance.

Name-calling

Geese, honking at an admiring man
Telling him to keep on walking,
"Go do your human thing"
Love your neighbor, talk to God.
Cackle cackle.

I used to walk in Belfast parks
Every Thursday for my health.
I got to know
Urban landscapes, including geese.

The geese need a talking to,
They fly in anxious exodus
Escaping to find
Still waters to boss in.
Honk, honk.

TIM HERE

You better duck
The glasses are raising again
Flagging Tim's name
Breaking down the tower
Of indifference
Flattening the sand grains of despair
Icy disregard
Gaudy articulations.

He has saved room for joy
With his hopeful talk
Purging with love
Presenting them with imageness
Offering tastes of grandeur,
Wearing out goodness
Weaving electric verbs with stated nouns,
Of meaning, purpose and value,
Letting us rest and reflect,
Leaving us full
For the next sunrise
Queuing up with smiles
In God's playground.
Hi, Tim here.

To Michael Whelan

How could you know Michael,
Your words of trees
Would sing down logging trails
Sit on telephone poles.

Prized Miramichi salmon
Inquire into idling fish nets,
Lighting pride inside Bathurst mines.
The woods, those soldiered tall of birch and pine
Claiming the calm, birthing a peace
Before wars' hooves and harm divide.

Your Erin tales, Sir Thomas More
Now battle computer lore to win or lose
Who our people were.

Those sainted names, you carved in praise
Still live at church, in ragged sleep.
Bring back our muse, our fiddled glee
Saturday night reality.

Let the Dungarvon utter
Its cursed moans, its just pangs
Memorized in attentive, one room school houses;
Who turns the key leaves a tale.

Doctor Visit

He landed,
Peeled back the door
In an explosive rush
Of anointed air,
And entered.

Cupping attentive ears
Spine need repair,
Flesh, muscle and nerves
Chorusing for wellness,
He courts the pain and counting every throb,
Carves a necklace of vertebrae
Sewn up in surprises of straightness.

Take off, by the elevator
Leaving pain meds
Scrawling,
"Life is such a dance,
Everyone needs the chance
To circle twice around,
In sickness and in health
Once lost, ever found."

THE LEPER
LUKE 5:12-16

"He has taught them with authority."
    A sermon on the mount, Christ's account
Teaching on life's meaning,
    About God's demand and man's demise.

Jesus walking down from up high level ground to earth
    The multitudes who heard flowed, massing to know
The ways and means of such a dream.

A man approached, a broach and sat down to slow
                the multitude.
    Allowed at once by all close
For he bore the brand of sure disease
    Pushed in face and disfigured hands.

The man was a leper
    Frosted fear and a cough-free distance
From all to accomplish
    For any defiled who bore skin's sores
Could not be neared lest it leap on us,
    And we all know his beleaguered woe
Is surely God's stain on past sinful claim.

But the leper then would not take a holiday and sat down
                                        at the parade's march.
    Worshipping the Lord canting in naked need,
"Lord if You want, You can make me clean."
Your word is your deed
    Your breath, the sin of action
Not now water to wine
    Not yet fish to fishes
But the mending of skin
    A silken contour for faith within.

Christ chose to say the words
    But willed in want to touch him first;
He stretched out His hand
    And closed the space that once was safe,
The two together, touching His hand on the
                                        cyst-soaked man.

He touched and all angelic caroled,
He touched and all false prophets cowered,
He touched and made him whole.

And Christ did say so men might see
    "I will, be you clean."

WINEMAKING
JOHN 2:1-12

The vines squat resigned idling in tea-time prattle
Anchored root-deep in soldiered rows
On cemetery green
Anticipating
Stretching out good mornings
Celebrating each courting breeze
In tendril shoots clinging and climbing
As high as the sky intends.

At all time prayerful, like monastic on bended knees
Decline to muse to be somehow grapes
For too few suns, too much rain
Or one short-ordered frost
Can cancer its course
Shrivel the dream gleaning
A famined taste aborted must.

But with each shoot side-stepping shade
A call for partners, Post and Vine,
And the green dances.
The leaves once curled in tight worry fists

Now extend their palms in a cogent vanity
And with no one around to claim they saw it so,
Limbs carrying pregnant boughs
Push berried delights of glassy reds and purples bright
Into the waiting arms of whistling sun.

Incarnate sway on chancel hillsides
Revelry with growing-pains
Spare changing rain
Maturing a season's long into —
Shingled balls of sugared marbles.

Leaving home bidding good-byes to parent limbs
Caught up in clusters
Tossed in transit to waiting press
Machine milked skins sloughed off
Residues kept for further processing —
Juices mix and join in exacting incubation
And
A wine of a kind
Sour to the cowering palette
Holding back to soften
Reflecting, musing
Tease the throat;
Encased asleep in aging cask.
Turning, searching
Invading lips
Communing.

And a wine
Aged eternity in waiting
Caroling in the jars for that instant time
To touch and stain the earthenware sides
From bowl down deep to spout and out
For a baptized birth water to wine —
Cabernet in Cana.

STORMY

Stormy
Life is dogging
Too much tears, too few smiles
Caroling with a friendly face.
Rainbow.

Stands tall
Paint on canvas
Reflecting God's image
Strokes of swirling truth mixed with love.
Artist.

THE SITTING SERAPHS

The sitting seraphs
Pant and wait the approaching,
Char unveiled armor.

An orange sunshine
Gleamed rays on setting sleep,
Fall on snoring seraphs.

God ascends at dawn
To color his creation
Orbs in tapestry.

Angels stretch their wings
Guardians of innocents
Warn fiery dragons.

HOMELESS

Home strapped on bent torso shoulders
Meaning wrapped in knots on a bedroll,
Streets stitch west, lengthening
Till lost in another nightfall,
Gauging warm and dry, or cold and wet.
No room at the inn

Sunrise elevating, offering the day
Baking visions of fresh bread and hot biscuits
Coating hopes, causing breath
Surely food for everyone.

But life in a photo album
Missing touch
Staging smiles
No room at the inn.

Traveler shuffles on a speeding footpath
As suits walk tightly and quickly by.
He talks to their striding faces,
They talk at a voiceless cell phone.

Feeling invisible
Standing out before us
In the embarrassment
Of a classless everything,
Wearing heartbeats like eggs in shell.

The stone rolls back
Invites travelers
Sit and stay, eat and sleep
Know and be known
At the inn.

DAY

Light announces day.
Hourglass stands
Loosing life with each drop of time
Over every grain of hope.

Liquid walls of rolling glass
Invade the land;
The sea insults the shore.

Storm clouds pine and sigh in complaint
Snap and bark in showers of argument,
Trees too stiff, too tall to dance
Etch and claw in beckoning earth.

Buds open in silent adoration
Fields of wheat sway their harvest song,
As winds play violin to the seated sun
And all look up to see, who dropped the rain.

Hourglass stills
Sand spent
Color sleeps
The symphony bows
Creation steeps.

POSTSCRIPT

THE LOOM. Marda and I have lived in North Belfast working and living in the mid Shankill Road community. We are pensioned faith-based volunteers from the United States. We do church and community relationship building. I am a pastor and a poet and Marda is a retired government program manager who networks people and projects into a tapestry.

We have been in North Belfast for nearly six years and we have been joined by an American colleague, a journalist who has written about C.S. Lewis. Jon follows the Christian Orthodox Church, neither a Roman Catholic nor a Protestant church. As The Loom we pray and build relationships so that the vision of Christian unity may encourage the world.

We are ordinary people whom God has equipped to bring good news and hope. We are grateful to the people of Northern Ireland who have welcomed us.

Thank you to my wife Marda, to my good friend Bill McKnight, to the writers especially Bill Jeffrey and Lynda Tavakoli. Thank you to Carolyne Gibson, my editor, and to McCall Gilfillan, Merve and Pen Jones for contributing your artwork. Thank you Reverend Jack Lamb for your faithfulness. Thank you to Carole Kane who encouraged our creativity. Final thanks goes to Ethel White the master weaver.

The proceeds from this book support charitable work to build the unity of believers to do no less than alleviate poverty and sustain world peace.

Ward Stothers
Belfast/Los Angeles/Berkeley
wardstothers@cten.org

The Dungarvon Press, Belfast
www.dungarvonpress.com

Made in the USA
San Bernardino, CA
14 March 2014